Francis Frith's
THE COTSWOLDS

PHOTOGRAPHIC MEMORIES

Francis Frith's
THE COTSWOLDS

◆

John Bainbridge

First published in the United Kingdom in 1999 by
Frith Book Company Ltd

Hardback Edition
ISBN 1-85937-099-3

Paperback Edition 2000
ISBN 1-85937-230-9

Hardback Reprinted in 2000

Paperback Reprinted in 2001

British Library Cataloguing in Publication Data

Francis Frith's The Cotswolds
John Bainbridge

Frith Book Company Ltd
Frith's Barn, Teffont,
Salisbury, Wiltshire SP3 5QP
Tel: +44 (0) 1722 716 376
Email: info@francisfrith.co.uk
www.francisfrith.co.uk

Printed and bound in Great Britain

CONTENTS

FRANCIS FRITH: *Victorian Pioneer*

FRANCIS FRITH, Victorian founder of the world-famous photographic archive, was a complex and multitudinous man. A devout Quaker and a highly successful Victorian businessman, he was both philosophic by nature and pioneering in outlook.

By 1855 Francis Frith had already established a wholesale grocery business in Liverpool, and sold it for the astonishing sum of £200,000, which is the equivalent today of over £15,000,000. Now a multi-millionaire, he was able to indulge his passion for travel. As a child he had pored over travel books written by early explorers, and his fancy and imagination had been stirred by family holidays to the sublime mountain regions of Wales and Scotland. 'What a land of spirit-stirring and enriching scenes and places!' he had written. He was to return to these scenes of grandeur in later years to 'recapture the thousands of vivid and tender memories', but with a different purpose. Now in his thirties, and captivated by the new science of photography, Frith set out on a series of pioneering journeys to the Nile regions that occupied him from 1856 until 1860.

INTRIGUE AND ADVENTURE

He took with him on his travels a specially-designed wicker carriage that acted as both dark-room and sleeping chamber. These far-flung journeys were packed with intrigue and adventure. In his life story, written when he was sixty-three, Frith tells of being held captive by bandits, and of fighting 'an awful midnight battle to the very point of surrender with a deadly pack of hungry, wild dogs'. Sporting flowing Arab costume, Frith arrived at Akaba by camel seventy years before Lawrence, where he encountered 'desert princes and rival sheikhs, blazing with jewel-hilted swords'.

During these extraordinary adventures he was assiduously exploring the desert regions bordering the Nile and patiently recording the antiquities and peoples with his camera. He was the first photographer to venture beyond the sixth cataract. Africa was still the mysterious 'Dark Continent', and Stanley and Livingstone's historic meeting was a decade into the future. The conditions for picture taking confound belief. He laboured for hours in his wicker dark-room in the sweltering heat of the desert, while the volatile chemicals fizzed dangerously in their trays. Often he was forced to work in remote tombs and caves where conditions were cooler. Back in London he exhibited his photographs and was 'rapturously cheered' by members of the Royal Society. His reputation as a photographer was made overnight. An eminent modern historian has likened their impact on the population of the time to that on our own generation of the first photographs taken on the surface of the moon.

VENTURE OF A LIFE-TIME

Characteristically, Frith quickly spotted the opportunity to create a new business as a specialist publisher of photographs. He lived in an era of immense and sometimes violent change. For the poor in the early part of Victoria's reign work was a drudge and the hours long, and people had precious little free time to enjoy themselves.

Most had no transport other than a cart or gig at their disposal, and had not travelled far beyond the boundaries of their own town or village. However, by the 1870s, the railways had threaded their way across the country, and Bank Holidays and half-day Saturdays had been made obligatory by Act of Parliament. All of a sudden the ordinary working man and his family were able to enjoy days out and see a little more of the world.

With characteristic business acumen, Francis Frith foresaw that these new tourists would enjoy having souvenirs to commemorate their days out. In 1860 he married Mary Ann Rosling and set out with the intention of photographing every city, town and village in Britain. For the next thirty years he travelled the country by train and by pony and trap, producing fine photographs of seaside resorts and beauty spots that were keenly bought by millions of Victorians. These prints were painstakingly pasted into family albums and pored over during the dark nights of winter, rekindling precious memories of summer excursions.

THE RISE OF FRITH & CO

Frith's studio was soon supplying retail shops all over the country. To meet the demand he gathered about him a small team of photographers, and published the work of independent artist-photographers of the calibre of Roger Fenton and Francis Bedford. In order to gain some understanding of the scale of Frith's business one only has to look at the catalogue issued by Frith & Co in 1886: it runs to some 670

pages, listing not only many thousands of views of the British Isles but also many photographs of most European countries, and China, Japan, the USA and Canada – note the sample page shown above from the hand-written *Frith & Co* ledgers detailing pictures taken. By 1890 Frith had created the greatest specialist photographic publishing company in the world, with over 2,000 outlets – more than the combined number that Boots and WH Smith have today! The picture on the right shows the *Frith & Co* display board at Ingleton in the Yorkshire Dales. Beautifully constructed with mahogany frame and gilt inserts, it could display up to a dozen local scenes.

POSTCARD BONANZA

The ever-popular holiday postcard we know today took many years to develop. In 1870 the Post Office issued the first plain cards, with a pre-printed stamp on one face. In 1894 they allowed other publishers' cards to be sent through the mail with an attached adhesive halfpenny stamp. Demand grew rapidly, and in 1895 a new size of postcard was permitted called the court card, but there was little room for illustration. In 1899, a year after Frith's death, a new card measuring 5.5 x 3.5 inches became the standard format, but it was not until 1902 that the divided back came into being, with address and message on one face and a full-size illustration on the other. *Frith & Co* were in the vanguard of postcard development, and Frith's sons Eustace and Cyril continued their father's monumental task, expanding the number of views offered to the public and recording more and more places in Britain, as the coasts and countryside were opened up to mass travel.

Francis Frith died in 1898 at his villa in Cannes, his great project still growing. The archive he created continued in business for another seventy years. By 1970 it contained over a third of a million pictures of 7,000 cities, towns and villages. The massive photographic record Frith has left to us stands as a living monument to a special and very remarkable man.

Frith's Archive: *A Unique Legacy*

FRANCIS FRITH'S legacy to us today is of immense significance and value, for the magnificent archive of evocative photographs he created provides a unique record of change in 7,000 cities, towns and villages throughout Britain over a century and more. Frith and his fellow studio photographers revisited locations many times down the years to update their views, compiling for us an enthralling and colourful pageant of British life and character.

We tend to think of Frith's sepia views of Britain as nostalgic, for most of us use them to conjure up memories of places in our own lives with which we have family associations. It often makes us forget that to Francis Frith they were records of daily life as it was actually being lived in the cities, towns and villages of his day. The Victorian age was one of great and often bewildering change for ordinary people, and though the pictures evoke an impression of slower times, life was as busy and hectic as it is today.

We are fortunate that Frith was a photographer of the people, dedicated to recording the minutiae of everyday life. For it is this sheer wealth of visual data, the painstaking chronicle of changes in dress, transport, street layouts, buildings, housing, engineering and landscape that captivates us so much today. His remarkable images offer us a powerful link with the past and with the lives of our ancestors.

TODAY'S TECHNOLOGY

Computers have now made it possible for Frith's many thousands of images to be accessed almost instantly. In the Frith archive today, each photograph is carefully 'digitised' then stored on a CD Rom. Frith archivists can locate a single photograph amongst thousands within seconds. Views can be catalogued and sorted under a variety of categories of place and content to the immediate benefit of researchers. Inexpensive reference prints can be created for them at the touch of a mouse button, and a wide range of books and other printed materials assembled and published for a wider, more general readership - in the next twelve months over a hundred Frith local history titles will be published! The

See Frith at www. francisfrith.co.uk

day-to-day workings of the archive are very different from how they were in Francis Frith's time: imagine the herculean task of sorting through eleven tons of glass negatives as Frith had to do to locate a particular sequence of pictures! Yet the archive still prides itself on maintaining the same high standards of excellence laid down by Francis Frith, including the painstaking cataloguing and indexing of every view.

It is curious to reflect on how the internet now allows researchers in America and elsewhere greater instant access to the archive than Frith himself ever enjoyed. Many thousands of individual views can be called up on screen within seconds on one of the Frith internet sites, enabling people living continents away to revisit the streets of their ancestral home town, or view places in Britain where they have enjoyed holidays. Many overseas researchers welcome the chance to view special theme selections, such as transport, sports, costume and ancient monuments.

We are certain that Francis Frith would have heartily approved of these modern developments, for he himself was always working at the very limits of Victorian photographic technology.

THE VALUE OF THE ARCHIVE TODAY

Because of the benefits brought by the computer, Frith's images are increasingly studied by social historians, by researchers into genealogy and ancestory, by architects, town planners, and by teachers and schoolchildren involved in local history projects. In addition, the archive offers every one of us a unique opportunity to examine the places where we and our families have lived and worked down the years. Immensely successful in Frith's own era, the archive is now, a century and more on, entering a new phase of popularity.

THE PAST IN TUNE WITH THE FUTURE

Historians consider the Francis Frith Collection to be of prime national importance. It is the only archive of its kind remaining in private ownership and has been valued at a million pounds. However, this figure is now rapidly increasing as digital technology enables more and more people around the world to enjoy its benefits.

Francis Frith's archive is now housed in an historic timber barn in the beautiful village of Teffont in Wiltshire. Its founder would not recognize the archive office as it is today. In place of the many thousands of dusty boxes containing glass plate negatives and an all-pervading odour of photographic chemicals, there are now ranks of computer screens. He would be amazed to watch his images travelling round the world at unimaginable speeds through network and internet lines.

The archive's future is both bright and exciting. Francis Frith, with his unshakeable belief in making photographs available to the greatest number of people, would undoubtedly approve of what is being done today with his lifetime's work. His photographs, depicting our shared past, are now bringing pleasure and enlightenment to millions around the world a century and more after his death.

THE COTSWOLDS – *An Introduction*

THE COTSWOLDS - it is an evocative name, which conjures up a delightful vision of the English countryside at its most pastoral: a landscape of rolling hills and meadows, quiet river banks, honey-stoned villages and bustling market towns. The Cotswolds are all of these and more, though the debate as to their exact boundary can be ferocious. It is best to interpret their geographical extent as generously as possible. Similarly, breaking up the area into descriptive regions is also difficult - any divisions proposed in this book are a matter of personal choice rather than anything definitive.

To travel through the Cotswolds is to wander through several thousand years of our history. This is a landscape largely created by man, with every passing civilisation leaving a mark. The end result we see today is a pleasing confirmation that the human race can sometimes complement nature rather than destroy it. Archaeologists tell us that these high wolds would have been densely settled even in Roman times, though the evidence of antiquity points to the hills and valleys being important to Neolithic man.

The Anglo-Saxons and Normans began the shaping of the towns and villages, with their generous market squares, taverns and fine wool churches. With the passing of the great religious houses of the district the riches of the wool trade were distributed more widely, to the benefit of local communities. It is impossible to underestimate just what a trade this was, both in its original form during the Middle Ages, when wool was England's greatest export, and later when the pioneers of the Industrial Revolution turned their attentions to the manufacture and mass-production of cloth.

Coming to terms with this long history is as much a delight for resident and visitor as the scenery itself - both are intertwined. The Cotswolds are a place to explore, escape into, and linger in. Such is the potency of their magic that visitors return again and again - or settle there permanently.

THE NAME

Originally the name Cotswold applied only to the area around the source of the River Windrush, and then spread south and west over hundreds of years. 'Wold' means hill, therefore to call the Cotswolds the 'Cotswold Hills' is a duplication. The 'Cot' may derive from the same source as 'cote' in Sheepcote - a place where sheep are enclosed, a very appropriate derivation for this neighbourhood. Locals suggest, as an alternative, that the area is named after a Saxon warlord called 'Cod' - Cod's Wold.

The Southern Cotswolds

To say that the southern Cotswolds were once the most heavily-industrialised parts of the region would be to give a false impression of the lie of the land. With the mechanisation of the cloth industry, the fast-flowing rivers around Stroud were used to power the mills which manufactured much of the world's broadcloth and other woollen goods. Huge stone buildings were erected to cater for the industrialisation of this traditional Cotswold trade, and cottages crept up the steep hillsides to accommodate the workers who flooded in from far and wide.

But the Cotswolds' contribution to the Industrial Revolution was extremely localised and on a minor scale when compared with the great industrial centres of Lancashire and the Black Country. The surrounding countryside was not overwhelmed by these activities. Stroud itself retains its attractive setting; the valleys and deep dark woodlands thereabouts more than compensate for the slightly urbanised feel of the old mill town. Much of the cloth industry has now disappeared, and the towns and villages that served it have spent much of the last half-century rediscovering and reinventing themselves. New industries such as tourism have developed, for this is a beautiful locality to explore and linger in.

Not all of the settlements in the southern Cotswolds found an importance in only the last two hundred years. Cirencester was the second most important town in Roman Britain after London. It prospered again in the Middle Ages as it exploited the wool industry, spurred on to giddy commercial heights by the monks of the great abbey which dominated the town. When Henry VIII despatched that particular religious house to the history books, merchant adventurers took over. Cirencester's wool church is an architectural reminder of how well they endowed their local community.

Some southern Cotswolds settlements avoided moving so dynamically with the times. There are still the villages and wilder countryside that the march of national history seems to have bypassed. All are extremely photogenic, with links to a quieter past: a reminder that not all of medieval England quite died with the coming of industry. Halt awhile in hamlets such as Duntisbourne Leer, plunge into the extensive woods around Cranham, stroll through the streets of Painswick in the quiet of evening when the tourists have left, or spend an afternoon in Slad, with a copy of Laurie Lee's 'Cider With Rosie' to hand, seeking out the scenes immortalised in that classic autobiography. That is the best way to get a feel for those parts of the southern Cotswolds that the Industrial Revolution missed.

AMBERLEY 1901 47357

Amberley straddles high ground to the south of Stroud, amid glorious Cotswold scenery. This old settlement achieved popularity during Victorian times as the setting for the then popular novel 'John Halifax, Gentleman'. Its author, Mrs Craik, lived at Rose Cottage.

BIBURY, THE CHURCH c1955 B530018

Bibury Church, situated in what William Morris considered to be 'the most beautiful village in England', shows much of its Saxon origins, though tempered with attractive Norman and Early English additions. The splendour of the tombs in the churchyard shows the wealth of the area in the days when wool was England's biggest export.

BIBURY, ARLINGTON MILL c1955 B530025

Though the present building is mostly 17th-century, a mill has existed on this site since Domesday. Arlington Mill served the locality as both a corn and cloth mill and has most recently been a countryside museum, with an excellent display about the life and works of William Morris.

BIBURY, ARLINGTON ROW c1960 B530002

This fine row of early 17th-century weavers' cottages is now owned by the National Trust. Bibury itself is an amalgamation of several earlier hamlets, which have all merged together to make the glorious architectural composition we see today.

BIBURY, THE RIVER c1960   B530031

BIBURY
The River c1960
The River Coln sweeps majestically through the village, a haunt for ducks and a place to watch large trout in the depths of the water. It was the combination of excellent grazing for sheep on the nearby hills and a fine water supply to power the mills that made villages such as Bibury rich, in the heyday of the woollen trade.

BIBURY
The Village Stores c1960
By the 1960s, Cotswold villages like Bibury had to cope with the large influx of visitors who came to admire the scenery. When this photograph was taken, double yellow lines had but recently arrived in an attempt to stop motorists obstructing the view of the very buildings they had come to see.

BIBURY, THE VILLAGE STORES c1960   B530029

BISLEY, HIGH STREET 1910 62697a

Bisley stands high on a hillside to the north of the River Frome; it has a wonderful assortment of winding streets and rooftops at different levels, as though the village has grown out of the landscape. It is a place to linger and explore, with every turn of a street revealing new delights.

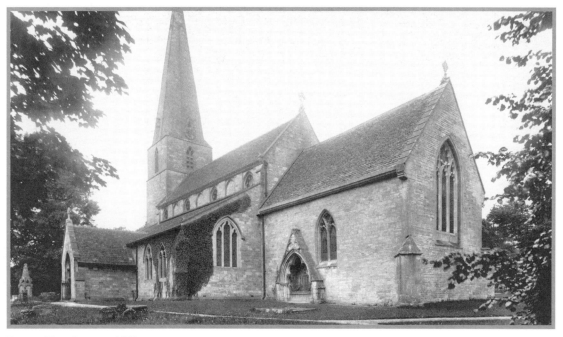

BISLEY, THE CHURCH 1910 62694

BISLEY, THE OLD BONE HOUSE 1910   62695

BISLEY
The Church 1910
The fine lines of Bisley Church show
that this is another village that earned its
wealth from the wool trade, its
magnificent spire declaring to the
neighbourhood the pride of its
benefactors - the wool merchants.

BISLEY
The Old Bone House 1910
In Bisley's churchyard is this strange
seated memorial, which covers the
original bone hole, where surplus human
remains, discovered by
gravediggers, would be interred. Legend
relates that several centuries ago the
village priest fell into the hole and died.
An outraged Pope decreed that no
burials would be permitted at Bisley for
two years. During that period the
village's deceased had to be carried some
miles to Bibury instead, where part of the
graveyard is still known as 'Bisley Piece'.

BISLEY, THE SEVEN SPRINGS 1910   62696

Below the village, seven springs spout a plentiful supply of water. These wells must have been used by locals for generations. The inscription above the springs reads 'Bless Ye The Lord, Praise Him, And Magnify'.

BUSSAGE, THE VILLAGE C1955 B259026

Hidden in woodland near Stroud, Bussage acquired fame in the 20th century as the home and workshop of the renowned glass engraver and stained glass artist Michael Dinkel.

CHALFORD, GENERAL VIEW 1890 25166
Not far from Stroud, the village of Chalford clings to the steep wooded hillside of the Golden Valley. Many of Chalford's streets are too narrow and steep to allow cars and are best explored on foot, much as the master-weavers of the cloth trade would have known them.

CHALFORD, THE CHURCH 1890 25169
Chalford's church is recent in origin compared to many in the Cotswolds: it was built in 1724, when the mills of the area were operating at maximum capacity, allowing some of their profits to be used to endow local buildings. This church was restored by the Victorians, and has some good carvings from that period inside.

CHALFORD, THE CHURCH 1900 45588

Chalford shows a degree of industrialisation at odds with the rest of the Cotswolds, and its hillsides are crammed with the workplaces and residences of mill workers. Most of the mills are now silent, dedicated to other uses, but the atmosphere of an industrial town persists.

CHALFORD, GENERAL VIEW 1900 45587

The mechanisation of the traditional cloth industry created the Chalford we see today. But other nearby Cotswold villages suffered as traditional methods were abandoned, making them unable to compete with newer technology. This may be why so many neighbouring villages appear to be frozen in time - there was little need and no money to construct new buildings.

CHALFORD, THE GOLDEN VALLEY 1910 62709
This was a Golden Valley in more senses than one.
Some industrialists made a fortune by opening mills
along the steep-sided valley that runs from Stroud to
near Cirencester. In autumn, when the trees turn
brown, the valley is golden in another way.

CHALFORD 1910 62713a
A donkey cart stands idle in one of Chalford's steep and narrow lanes. Carts such as this were used to bring wool down to the mills from local farms. Having a photograph taken was still a novel enough experience to attract a crowd.

CHALFORD, ON THE CANAL 1910 62712

Cloth manufactured in Chalford was transported throughout Britain by way of the Thames and Severn Canal, which functioned as a working waterway until the 1950s. The canal gave access to the ports of Bristol and London, and much of the cloth was shipped onwards to far-flung corners of the British Empire.

CIRENCESTER, MARKET PLACE 1898 40965
In Roman times Cirencester, Corinium Dubunnorum,
was the second most important town in Britain after
London, standing near the Roman roads of Akeman
Street, the Fosse Way, Ermine Street and the older
Icknield Way. Much of south-west England was
administered from here. It revived as a Saxon
settlement, but it did not become prominent again
until the emergence of the wool trade.

CIRENCESTER, CASTLE STREET 1898 40971

Much of the woollen industry, by which Cirencester prospered, was organised by the monks of the great abbey which was completed during the reign of Henry II. His successor Henry VIII dissolved the abbey, and only the Spital Gateway remains. The wool industry was delivered into the hands of merchant adventurers, who built the huge perpendicular wool church that now dominates the town's market square.

CIRENCESTER, GLOUCESTER STREET 1898 42362

Cirencester is another Cotswold town best explored on foot, not least since traffic has increased substantially since this photograph was taken over a century ago. Fine architecture from all periods survives and the town still prospers, thanks to the shoppers who arrive each week on market days.

CIRENCESTER, THE PARK, OXEN TEAM 1898 40986
Cirencester Park, famous now for polo matches, lies to the west of the town. Tradition relates that the poet Alexander Pope had a hand in its design. The extensive grounds are still privately owned, though walkers and riders are usually welcomed if approaching from the town end.

CIRENCESTER, THE HOUNDS 1898 40987
A hunt meet within the 3000 acres of Cirencester park. The park was originally designed as a leisure and sporting estate by the first Lord Bathurst in the early 1700s.

COLESBOURNE, GENERAL VIEW c1960 C453008

Colesbourne stands halfway between Cirencester and Cheltenham, astride a busy main road. This is a land of meadow and wold. Once the visitor is away from the road, he finds a peaceful and seldom-visited landscape awaiting exploration.

COLESBOURNE, LOWER HILCOT c1960 C453011

An ancient ford and footbridge, an abandoned cartwheel, and the splash of running water over a tiny weir - this delightful photograph of two stone cottages and their attractive gardens reminds us that the countryside maintained a timeless air even in the hurry of the 20th century.

COLESBOURNE
The Colesbourne Inn c1960

The Colesbourne Inn, conveniently halfway between Cheltenham and Cirencester, probably had its origin as a place of refreshment for horse-drawn coach passengers. Local legend relates the tales of several highwaymen who plied their trade along this profitable route.

◆

COLESBOURNE
The Post Office c1960

Here we see a post office added to an older building, as so often happened in the Cotswolds, serving as a village store to both locals and travellers on the busy main road. Colesbourne is too often rushed through by the modern motorist. It is worth exploring.

COLESBOURNE, THE COLESBOURNE INN c1960   C453006

COLESBOURNE, THE POST OFFICE c1960   C453005

CRANHAM WOODS 1907 59066
A horse-drawn carriage takes a journey into the extensive woodlands of Cranham, Brockworth and Buckholt. A century later this is still one of the most beautiful stretches of countryside in England. In the autumn the beech trees of Cranham turn a glorious gold, attracting visitors from far and wide.

CRANHAM WOODS 1907 59068

The villages of Cranham and Sheepscombe border wild countryside of woodland and common. Cranham shows its appreciation of the wool money which helped pay for the church by having a pair of wool shears carved on the tower. Sheepscombe - its very name a reminder of the old industry - features in Laurie Lee's memorable autobiography 'Cider With Rosie'.

CRANHAM WOODS c1955 C179307a

The undulating countryside of woodland, common and meadow tempts many a motorist to pause by the roadside to admire the scenery. But the woods are best explored by the network of footpaths and bridleways threading between the local villages.

CRANHAM WOODS, PRINKNASH ABBEY c1965 C179031

Prinknash (pronounced Prinnage) Abbey is for the most part a very modern building, rising stark from the valley. But the old manor house is a reminder that this is a very old site, dating back to the 16th century. Benedictines returned to Prinknash in the mid-20th century, establishing the world-famous pottery which can be visited.

CRANHAM WOODS, VIEW TOWARDS THE CHURCH c1965 C179049

This view shows the variety of scenery in this delightful part of the Cotswolds. The mixture of woodland, common land and meadows would have provided everything villagers would have needed for survival in the Middle Ages.

CRANHAM WOODS C1965 C179051

Many consider the countryside around Cranham and Sheepscombe to be the finest in the Cotswolds, though others champion distant parts. A diplomatic solution is to say that the bit of the Cotswolds you are in at the time is the best!

DUNTISBOURNE ABBOTS, THE VILLAGE C1960 D161009

Duntisbourne Abbots was once the property of the Abbots of Gloucester; it is the northernmost of a string of villages lining the River Dunt. Its churchyard, shadowed by the saddle-backed church tower, is one of the prettiest in the Cotswolds, and a good place to linger on a peaceful day.

DUNTISBOURNE ABBOTS
The Ford c1960

A car negotiates a long ford by the village. This would have been a familiar route for Dr Matthew Baillie, the eminent physician who attended George III during his long years of mental illness.

◆

DUNTISBOURNE ABBOTS
The Youth Hostel c1960

The Youth Hostels Movement was founded by Richard Schurrman in 1907, and was rapidly and enthusiastically introduced into Britain. Many impressive buildings were acquired as hostels, such as this stately house at Duntisbourne Abbots. A hostelling tour on foot or bicycle is still one of the best ways to explore the Cotswolds.

DUNTISBOURNE ABBOTS, THE FORD c1960 D161011

DUNTISBOURNE ABBOTS, THE YOUTH HOSTEL c1960 D161001

DUNTISBOURNE LEER, THE VILLAGE c1965 D245013
Just along the road from Duntisbourne Abbots is the village of Duntisbourne Leer, named after the great Normandy Abbey at Lire which once owned the manor. Not much more than a large hamlet, Duntisbourne Leer is yet another photogenic and thoroughly charming Cotswold village.

FAIRFORD, HIGH STREET FROM THE CHURCH c1955 F145008
In the modern age, Fairford in Gloucestershire is associated with aircraft. Concorde made its maiden flight from the airfield nearby, and most visitors only come once a year for the International Air Show. This is a pity, for Fairford boasts a great deal of fine architecture, with many Georgian and Regency buildings.

FAIRFORD, THE CHURCH AND THE MILL C1955 F145001

The joy of Fairford is its ornate wool church, built in the latter part of the 15th century by John Tame, a wealthy cloth merchant. No other church in England boasts such a wonderful array of early stained glass, 28 examples in all, telling the Christian story from the Creation to the Day of Judgement.

FAIRFORD, RIVER COLN C1955 F145009

Fairford was the birthplace of the 19th-century Christian reformer and hymn-writer John Keble, who would often walk along the banks of the River Coln seeking inspiration for his verse. His book 'The Christian Year' led to the birth of the Oxford Movement, and many of his lyrics are still sung in Cotswold churches.

FAIRFORD, THE BULL INN c1955 F145014

FAIRFORD
The Bull Inn c1955
The Bull Inn is one of a large number of coaching inns established in Fairford to service the coaching trade, for this attractive town stands on what was one of southern England's most important coaching routes.

INGLESHAM
Little Holme Youth Hostel c1955
From cottage to mansion, the Youth Hostels Association adapted a wide range of buildings for use by their increasing membership. The hostel at Inglesham was modest compared to some, but still provided all the needs of food and bed for the weary Cotswold explorer.

INGLESHAM, LITTLE HOLME YOUTH HOSTEL c1955 I26001

LECHLADE, HIGH STREET c1960 L147042

Situated near where Oxfordshire, Berkshire and Wiltshire meet is the pretty village of Lechlade, with its fine array of Georgian houses. The church, with its distinctive spire, dates from the 15th century, and dominates the town's market square.

LECHLADE, THE WHARF c1960 L147101

Lechlade stands at the confluence of three rivers, the Leach, the Coln and the Thames - called here the Isis. It was from here that the stone used for the dome of St Pauls Cathedral, quarried nearby at Taynton, was loaded onto barges and transported downstream to London.

LECHLADE, THE ROUND HOUSE c1960 L147026
This old Round House was built for the use of the canal lengthmen, who maintained certain sections, or lengths, of the Thames and Severn canal, which started near Inglesham, close to Lechlade.

MINCHINHAMPTON, THE CHURCH FROM SW 1901 47350
Holy Trinity Church at Minchinhampton has a highly distinctive tower, standing sentinel over the grey limestone of this hilltop town. The church dates back to the 12th century, and is adorned by some beautiful stained glass and a fine collection of brasses.

MINCHINHAMPTON, THE MARKET HALL 1901 47348
Minchinhampton's very fine Market Hall dates from 1698, and demonstrates the early prosperity of this important wool town. The nearby post office is surely one of the most delightful of such buildings anywhere in England, situated as it is in a genuine Queen Anne building.

MINCHINHAMPTON, OUTSIDE THE TOWN 1901 47355
Minchinhampton is an excellent centre for the tourist to the Cotswolds, ideal for motorist, cyclist or walker. Even in a car-ridden age it is still possible to find country lanes safe for pedestrians to stroll peacefully along.

MINCHINHAMPTON, THE GOLF LINKS, 3RD HOLE 1910 62692a
Minchinhampton golf course is situated on the edge of the common land which borders the town. There is a marvellous all-round viewpoint on these 600 acres, now mostly owned by the National Trust.

MINCHINHAMPTON, VIEW FROM FORWOOD c1955 M83045

During the Iron Age, Minchinhampton was a residential area for the Celtic Dobunni tribe, who held sway across this strategically-important high ground prior to the Roman occupation. But many of the dykes, barrows and standing stones near to the town are probably even older.

NAILSWORTH, FROM ROCKNESS 1904 53110

Apart from a plethora of now silent industrial mills, now mostly put to other uses, the steep lanes of Nailsworth are lined with the cottages of former cloth workers. The streets are steep. The steepest, the appropriately named Nailsworth Ladder, is probably 1 in 2.

NAILSWORTH, WATLEDGE 1904 53113a

The majority of Nailsworth's buildings are less than 250 years old, built for the workers who had a hard life in the local mills. Apart from the local stone, it would be easy to imagine that you had wandered away from the Cotswolds into a Pennine mill town, such is the industrial atmosphere.

NAILSWORTH, GENERAL VIEW 1890 25172

Nailsworth may not be the most attractive town in the Cotswolds, but the student of industrial archaeology will find it a fascinating place to visit. For it was here that the ancient cloth trade of the area enjoyed a mechanised renaissance at the time of the Industrial Revolution.

NAILSWORTH, NEWMARKET 1904 53114

Despite its industrial base, the surrounding Cotswolds countryside beckoned for any workers who had some precious spare time to get away from the noise, dust and long hours of work.

NAILSWORTH, BRIDGE STREET c1955 N1004

Nailsworth's shops have always tended towards the functional rather than the decorative. Davis' shop on the left boasts that not only has it a thousand razors on display and carries out watch and jewellery repairs, but also provides the services of an 'optician qualified by examination'.

NAILSWORTH, THE TROUT HATCHERIES c1960 N1006

With the demise of the cloth industry, towns such as Nailsworth had to find alternative activities. The clear water of the Cotswold rivers and streams proved ideal for commercial fish farming.

NORTHLEACH, MARKET SQUARE c1955 N125013

Northleach is a delightful town, easily missed with the construction of its recent bypass. As with so many Cotswolds settlements, it made its fortune in the wool trade and still shows off the grandeur of those rich and heady days. The Market Square is overlooked by what is arguably the finest wool church in a countryside full of those magnificent buildings.

NORTHLEACH, UNION HOTEL AND HIGH STREET N125014

Northleach's High Street has a very varied mixture of architectural styles for a Cotswold town, including half-timbered houses. The scale of most of the buildings is dictated by the original Burgage Plots - the original amount of ground plot leased out by the early landowners, the monks of Gloucester Abbey.

NORTHLEACH, HIGH STREET 1956 N125035

At one end of High Street are the remains of Northleach's model prison, constructed under the guidance of Sir George Onesiphorus Paul, High Sheriff of Gloucestershire, in 1792. It was an enlightened establishment for its day. Some of its buildings have now been incorporated into the local countryside museum.

PAINSWICK CHURCH, NORTH SIDE 1890 25181

Painswick - the 'Queen of the Cotswolds' - is situated amid glorious woodland high on the western side of the wolds. Its narrow winding streets have a Dickensian feel, and but for the hum of traffic, it would be easy to imagine yourself back in more gracious times.

SLAD, THE VILLAGE 1910 62707

Immortalised by Laurie Lee in his autobiography 'Cider With Rosie', Slad and its wooded valley is known throughout the world by millions of readers who have never been there. We may be thankful that the village has managed to avoid the worst excesses of 20th-century development and that it is much as it was during Lee's boyhood.

SLAD, THE VALLEY 1910 62708

Slad is not the most beautiful village in the Cotswolds. Its setting is not the most spectacular, compared to some of its neighbours. But it does look as though it really belongs to the setting it has. It is a place of pilgrimage for admirers of Laurie Lee's writings - and a delightful day out for anyone.

Stroud, General View 1900 45579
Britain's most important centre for the manufacture of
broadcloth, this mill town sprawls across its wide
valley, a huge piece of industrialisation in a wonderfully
natural setting. It says a lot for the beauty and resilience
of the Cotswolds that the location has not been
overwhelmed by the urbanisation of an industrial age.

STROUD, BOWBRIDGE 1890 25152

With the decline of the cloth trade a number of other industries utilised the old buildings, including piano manufacture. The local museum has an excellent section detailing the rise and fall of the Cotswold cloth trade, and much about the important archaeology of the area.

STROUD, RODBOROUGH FORT 1890 25162A

By exploring the high ground around the town it is possible to gain some idea of the scale of industrialisation around Stroud. The eye is drawn further afield to the distant Severn Estuary, the Black Mountains of Wales and Exmoor.

STROUD, THE THRUPP 1900 45586

Probably only in the 19th century was Stroud and its outlying settlements considered to be properly in the Cotswolds. The scenery here is certainly different to the higher areas to the north and east; the Stroud valley and its neighbouring hills are lower and much more wooded.

STROUD, THRUPP AND MONTSERRAT 1910 62682

While the steep and winding streets around the Stroud Valley were hazardous to horse-drawn transport, they were a real challenge to the early motor car, which was limited in power and had dubious brakes.

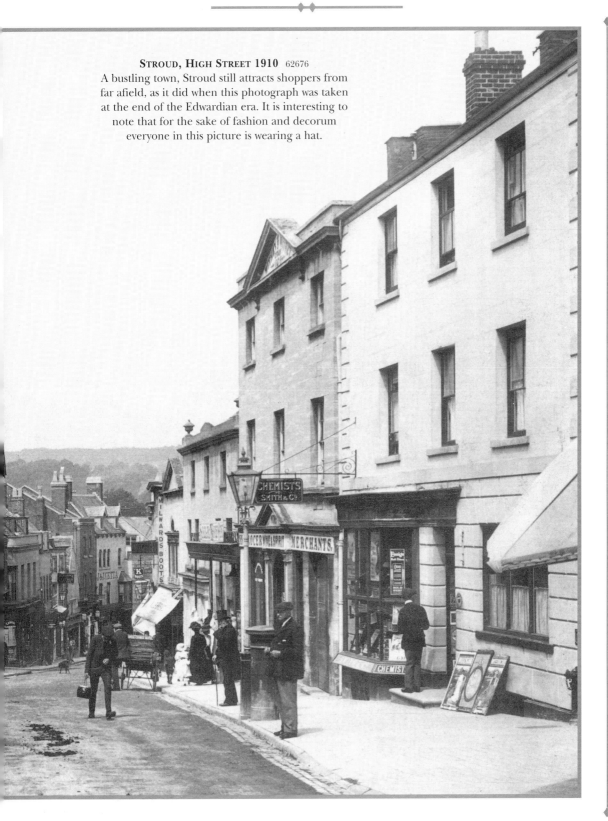

STROUD, HIGH STREET 1910 62676
A bustling town, Stroud still attracts shoppers from far afield, as it did when this photograph was taken at the end of the Edwardian era. It is interesting to note that for the sake of fashion and decorum everyone in this picture is wearing a hat.

STROUD, KING STREET 1910 62677
The prosperity of a mill town is reflected
by the huge variety of shops in these
photographs of Stroud, an example of
how industry supports other trades if
economic conditions are favourable. But
many traders were to suffer with the
decline of the cloth industry.

STROUD, KING STREET 1925 77562

Omnibus and bicycle opened up the outside world to many Cotswold villages. For the first time it was possible for shoppers to go into towns like Stroud on a regular basis. This increase in trade helped tide many of Stroud's shops over during the depressions of the 20th century.

STROUD, HIGH STREET c1955 S224010

By the 1950s many of the locally-owned small shops were giving way to familiar chain stores, though the streets remained relatively free of motor traffic.

STROUD, GLOUCESTER STREET c1955 S224021a

A policeman walks up through the streets to begin point duty. In the 1950s. Cycle shops still thrive, despite motor cars becoming affordable to a wider range of society. There are still outlets for buying and hiring bicycles in Stroud. There are few better forms of transport for touring the Cotswolds.

STROUD, HIGH STREET c1955 S224023a
Looking in the opposite direction to photograph No S224021 we see the same policeman directing traffic at the junction of High Street and Gloucester Street. A short walk from this spot will bring the sightseer to the Subscription Rooms, a handsome 19th-century building which now houses the Tourist Information Centre.

STROUD, RODBOROUGH COMMON c1960 S224082

Rodborough Common, owned by the National Trust, is a fine walk out from the south-west of Stroud. The fort on the summit was built in 1761 as a pleasure house by George Hawker, a local cloth dyer, and reconstructed by the Victorians.

TETBURY, CHURCH STREET c1949 T155027

Tetbury lies near the boundary of Gloucestershire and Wiltshire on the long stretch of high road between Stroud and Malmesbury. It has achieved fame in the last few years by becoming a royal town, for the Prince of Wales lives nearby at Highgrove.

TETBURY, GENERAL VIEW c1955   T155018

TETBURY, ST MARY'S CHURCH, WEST STREET c1955   T155017

TETBURY
General View c1955
Tetbury is one of the statelier towns of
the southern Cotswolds, overlooking a
tributary of the River Avon. Its location
prevented it from being despoiled by the
industrialists of the 19th century.
Tetbury retains all the charms of a
market town from the time of
the Stuarts.

TETBURY
St Mary's Church, West Street c1955
St Mary's church, with its tall and
distinctive spire, is a prominent
landmark for much of Tetbury. This
church was built late for the Cotswolds,
its gothic splendour dating only from
the late 18th century. Local tradition
alleges that Tetbury's newer church of
St Saviour's not far away was built for the
poor of the town, after wealthy
parishioners monopolised the box pews
in the original church.

TETBURY, THE MARKET PLACE c1955 T155024

Tetbury's 17th-century Market House is similar to other such buildings in the Cotswolds, except that the upper storey served as the town hall. The Market House is now well-used for local markets, sales and antique fairs.

TETBURY, BATH BRIDGE c1955 T155031

As a reminder of Tetbury's wool trade heritage, an annual woolsack race is held up the town's steep Gunstool Hill, each competitor carrying a burden of wool weighing 65 pounds.

TETBURY, CHIPPING STEPS c1955 T155038a
The old Chipping Steps lead down to the Cirencester Road from The Chipping, the original site of Tetbury Market. In medieval times a monastery covered much of the adjoining area, though little remains.

WOODCHESTER, GENERAL VIEW 1890 25173

Lying deep in a long valley, Woodchester is often missed by visitors to the Cotswolds, but should not be: it has an attractive curved main street, and some charming old cottages. The wiser tourist explores the village or sits to admire the outlook from higher ground, as this person did in 1890.

WOODCHESTER, THE CHURCH 1890 25174

Woodchester's church, with its dramatic and challenging lines, was designed and built by the notable architect Teulon in 1863-4. A prominent monument inside commemorates Wedgwood Allen of the Royal Flying Corps as a knight in armour.

WOODCHESTER, THE MONASTERY AND ROMAN CATHOLIC CHURCH 1900 45592
Woodchester has two monasteries, for Dominican and Franciscan monks respectively. Their Victorian buildings make a dramatic addition to an otherwise quiet and rolling landscape.

WOODCHESTER, THE VALLEY AND THE MONASTERY 1910 62684
Here we see a monastic landscape that seems more in keeping with the Middle Ages than 1910. In the days before motor traffic penetrated the quiet Cotswold lanes, this remained a remote and tranquil landscape.

WOODCHESTER, THE VALLEY 1910 62685

Beneath Woodchester's older churchyard was discovered one of the most important Roman villa sites in Britain. On the floor of its main hall the antiquarian Samuel Lyson found the Orpheus Pavement, a one and a half million-piece mosaic, probably created using local stone. It is not open to view, but a reproduction can be seen at Wooton-Under-Edge.

WOODCHESTER, THE VALLEY 1910 62686

Woodchester is surrounded by high ground and woodlands, all worth an exploratory walk in any direction. Selsey Common is a popular place for picnics, and Rodborough Common a windswept location for rambles and rides. All of the hilltops offer extensive views over the southern Cotswolds.

Cheltenham - The Western Gateway

THERE ARE THOSE who would argue that Cheltenham is not a true Cotswold town, and that this refined and carefully-planned city is geographically an intruder from the Vale of Gloucester. Cheltenham certainly seems at first glance to have little in common with those towns and villages high up on the wolds with their deep valleys, woodlands, meadows, grazing sheep, and buildings that look as though some wild act of geology threw them out of the landscape.

But few would dispute that Cheltenham has long earned its title as the Cotswolds' western gateway. The high viewpoint of Cleeve Hill, popularly regarded as the edge of the wolds, stands proudly above the town, with wide views across the valley of the river Severn to Wales. And many of Cheltenham's buildings are constructed from a similar honey-gold stone familiar to anyone who has explored the loftier landscape to the east of the city.

Cheltenham has, in any case, not always been the fashionable spa we see today. Three hundred years ago, it was a not very distinctive Cotswold village, visited mostly by shepherds with their flocks, stage coaches and sundry travellers on the way to somewhere else. It enjoyed little reputation beyond its fame as a village at the back of beyond. Then the future spa town's first mineral spring was discovered in 1715 by someone with time on their hands, who observed the watering habits of the local pigeons, who always seemed so fat and full of life. A pump room was constructed in 1738, and towards the end of the 18th century King George III gave the growing town the royal seal of approval by taking the waters. Business boomed, and when the town of Cheltenham Spa became a city its grateful citizens incorporated a pigeon into its crest.

Clearly, the old Cheltenham could not provide either the ambience or the facilities to cater for its new upmarket clientele. A calculated campaign of redesign and rebuilding was inaugurated, and this building boom gave us the beautiful and elegant Cheltenham Spa we see today, with its wide avenues, handsome terraces and luxury villas.

The 19th century saw the town expand rapidly as retired empire builders, colonial civil servants and pensioned military officers sought refuge there. Those who were still on active service in far-flung corners of the globe sent their children to Cheltenham, establishing the town's reputation as a centre for education.

Cheltenham is still a busy town with its modern industries, world-famous music and literature festivals, and the National Hunt racecourse - home of the Cheltenham Gold Cup. For the explorer of the western Cotswolds it is a perfect touring centre. Many have begun their love affair with this fascinating and historic region at Cleeve Hill, the dramatic backdrop to Cheltenham and its valley. There are few better places to start.

BISHOP'S CLEEVE, THE CHURCH c1955 B531030
Bishop's Cleeve has now become something of a small town, a dormitory for nearby Cheltenham, but it still has an attractive setting under the slopes of Cleeve Hill. Its fine church was mostly built in the 17th century, though some Norman features remain. The nearby rectory dates back seven hundred years, and part of the church's old tithe barn has now been absorbed into the village hall.

BISHOP'S CLEEVE, THE VILLAGE c1955 B531002
Despite some widespread demolition in the 1950s, many lovely old buildings remain in Bishop's Cleeve. The village dates back to at least Saxon times. In the 8th century Aldred, a local king, gave land for a church to be dedicated to St Michael the Archangel.

CHELTENHAM, THE DEVIL'S CHIMNEY 1901 47256
This tall limestone pillar stands above the quarries on Leckhampton Hill, not far from Cheltenham. Much of the stone for the spa town came from this area, and the Devil's Chimney is probably a result of quarrying as well as erosion. There are wonderful views from here across the plain of the River Severn.

CHELTENHAM, THE PROMENADE 1901 47261a

Three hundred years ago Cheltenham was just another stone village on the edge of the Cotswolds. It fortunes changed in 1715 when a mineral spring was discovered. Within a few years fashionable society began to arrive to take the waters.

CHELTENHAM, HIGH STREET 1901 47265
Not every visitor was impressed by the elegance of
Cheltenham Spa. William Cobbett described the town
in 'Rural Rides' as 'a nasty ill-looking place', full of
"East India plunderers, West Indian floggers, English
tax-gorgers...gluttons, drunkards and debauchers of all
descriptions, female as well as male'. It was certainly
true that fashionable resorts did attract the
disreputable in this way.

CHELTENHAM, LONDON ROAD 1906 54321

Cheltenham quickly became a retirement home for officers and colonial administrators, who occupied its Regency terraces and purpose-built villas. In more recent years Cheltenham has established an enviable reputation for fashion and design, for music and literature festivals, and for National Hunt racing on the nearby racecourse.

CHELTENHAM, LECKHAMPTON ROAD 1923 73502

Gustav Holst was born in Cheltenham in 1874, attending the local grammar school before becoming one of England's greatest composers. Long before he achieved fame from 'The Planets' and 'Egdon Heath', he composed pieces of music inspired by the delightful Cotswold scenery.

CHELTENHAM, THE PROMENADE 1931 83808

Near to the Promenade is Pittville Park, where Joseph Pitt established a classically-designed pump room in the 19th century - the last to be built in the spa town. Visitors can still take the waters within, while admiring the fine collection of Regency costumes on display.

CHELTENHAM, THE COLLEGE 1901 47270

Cheltenham has become a byword for public school education in England. Its College for boys, situated on the road to Bath, was built in the 1840s in the popular Gothic revival style. The nearby Cheltenham Ladies' College was founded by the formidable Victorian educationalist Miss Beale.

CHELTENHAM
THE COLLEGE PLAYING FIELDS 1907 59038
Even today the College boasts an annual summer
cricket festival, in the best public school tradition. At
the height of the British Empire, the colleges took in
the children of military officers and civil servants
posted to far-flung corners of Queen Victoria's realm.

CHELTENHAM, THE CENTRE 1960 C75129a

By the 1960s, chain stores had become established, even in fashionable Cheltenham. Happily, many individual shops of fine character selling a wide variety of goods have survived.

CLEEVE HILL, GENERAL VIEW 1907 59055

Cleeve Hill is the western edge of the Cotswolds, and at over a thousand feet the highest point. In the far distance are the hills of Wales, the Mendips and Exmoor. Nearer are the Vale of Gloucester, Cheltenham and the flood plains of the River Severn.

CLEEVE HILL, GENERAL VIEW 1907 59054

This distinctive and windswept plateau, often the first place in the Cotswolds to catch the westerly rains and gales, is ancient common land, where generations of local farmers and cottagers had the right to graze and gather fuel.

CLEEVE HILL, GENERAL VIEW 1907 59057

CLEEVE HILL
General View 1907
Cleeve Hill should properly be climbed
on foot from either Bishop's Cleeve or
Winchcombe to get the full effect of its
dominance over the plain below.

◆

CLEEVE HILL
Wash Pool Farm 1907
Below the summit of Cleeve Hill is agricultural land worked since the dawn of
time. A number of Cotswold farms occu-
py sites used by farmers since
before Domesday.

CLEEVE HILL, WASH POOL FARM 1907 59060

CLEEVE HILL, GENERAL VIEW 1931 83824
Cleeve Hill is at its most impressive when climbed on a clear day at dawn or sunset, avoiding the weekend crowds who take the easy option of driving up to the car park near the summit.

CLEEVE HILL, GOLF LINKS 1931 83825
The slopes of the Cotswolds have attracted golfers since Victorian times, and some twenty clubs now ring the area. The links on Cleeve Hill are popular with players from nearby Cheltenham, offering not only a challenging game but good views.

CLEEVE HILL, GENERAL VIEW C1955 C115008
Cleeve Hill has now been designated as a Site of Special Scientific Interest because of the variety of flora and fauna on its unenclosed common land and the rich supply of fossils to be found in its limestone outcrops and old quarries.

PRESTBURY, THE CHURCH 1901 47300
Prestbury, close to Cheltenham Racecourse, has the reputation of being one of the most haunted villages in England. A cavalier hurries through the streets, a monk haunts shady corners of the village, and a violent phantom hovers to trap the unwary - leaving them all aside, Prestbury is a pleasant place for a stroll.

PRESTBURY, THE VILLAGE 1907 59051a
As the home of such a famous racecourse, Prestbury has been the training ground for many famous racehorses.
The tram and cyclists here are heading up the steep ascent of Cleeve Hill, which is not far from the village.

The Northern Cotswolds

THE NORTHERN COTSWOLDS are a land little changed by time. Take away the ubiquitous motor car from the village streets, and it is quite possible to gaze at the honey-stoned cottages, the winding lanes and ancient churches and imagine yourself back in a very different age.

There is little of the industrialisation of the south, and no large towns such as Cheltenham in the west. The towns of the north and east tend to be small, functional places, owing their original prosperity to the wool trade, but having changed remarkably little since. Burford, Chipping Norton, Stow-on-the-Wold and Winchcombe are old settlements, whose names resonate through English history; some were important in Saxon times, others show signs of the Norman yoke, or battle damage from the Civil War.

They survived, and still do today, as market towns - places where it is still possible to hear the Cotswold burr spoken among the myriad accents of visitors from further afield.

The villages are a delight, some of the prettiest in England. Their breathtaking beauty and harmony tempt the traveller to stay for ever. It is easy to understand just why the locals are fiercely loyal to the places where they live. Even in the obvious tourist traps of Bourton-on-the-Water, with its collection of bridges and river scenery, or the Slaughters and the Swells with their picture postcard joys, the attractiveness has remained undiminished, even with their need to cater for so many admirers.

Most villages grew up along the banks of rivers and streams which flow idly, compared to the swifter waters of the south. Old mills

survive, powered by water, which serviced the wool and cloth trade as well as the pressing agricultural needs of local communities for centuries. Many streams wind splendidly through the midst of town and village, giving a place to stroll, linger, or just feed the ducks. They have exquisite, evocative names like Windrush and Evenlode - as poetic in name as they are delightful to follow.

Beyond the settlements and river valleys are the high wolds, sheep-grazing land for thousands of years. This is a landscape more ancient than the oldest buildings in the valleys below. It was old when the Romans came, as ancient monuments such as the Rollright Stones suggest. It is a place where humanity has always lived in harmony with the land and nature. Some of the tracks probably date back to that time, making the Roman roads which criss-cross the region look recent by comparison.

This is a pastoral land of wide horizons, where the sky seems to touch the distant hilltops, an enthralling world often deserted except for the grazing sheep and circling birds.

ASCOTT-UNDER-WYCHWOOD, THE VILLAGE C1955 A140006
Along the Evenlode, that gentle Cotswold stream, stands a string of villages all 'under Wychwood', that ancient wood that still remains one of the most extensive stretches of woodland in Oxfordshire, but which in earlier times was a substantial forest. With its neighbouring village Shipton-Under-Wychwood, Ascott had a reputation for harbouring poachers in earlier centuries.

ASCOTT-UNDER-WYCHWOOD, LANGLEY MILL c1955 A140011
The streams that flow into the Evenlode were an asset for the mills serving agriculture and the cloth trade. This old mill at Ascott-Under-Wychwood is a fine example of how substantial these buildings could be, built as they were from strong Cotswold stone.

BOURTON-ON-THE-WATER, THE FOOTBRIDGE 1948 B392035
Bourton-on-the-Water is probably the most popular tourist haunt in the Cotswolds. It deserves its popularity. This stretch of the pretty little River Windrush, the collection of low stone bridges, and a fine village of Cotswold stone, all combine to make a memorable day out.

BOURTON-ON-THE-WATER, THE VILLAGE c1955 B392038

Its accessibility from the towns and cities of the Midlands has made Bourton a favourite day out. The village scarcely seems despoiled by having so many admirers. It is still possible to find a quiet corner to feed the ducks, a pleasant shop to browse in, and an ancient inn to enjoy a lunchtime meal.

BOURTON-ON-THE-WATER, FEEDING THE DUCKS c1955 B392047

Bourton Bridge, which carries the busy main road past the village, was the first of the town's many bridges; the original structure dated back to Roman times and was designed to aid the legions as they marched down the Fosse Way. The little bridges that delight the photographer are much more recent, the oldest being about 250 years old.

BOURTON-ON-THE-WATER, THE MODEL VILLAGE c1955 B392051
Rather like Gulliver in Lilliput, the visitor finds an exact likeness of Bourton-on-the-Water in its famous model village. The model village itself has a replica model village and that model village a smaller model village....and so on and so on.

BOURTON-ON-THE-WATER, THE STUDIO CAFE c1955 B392056
The village teashop is a wonderful British tradition. The joy of Bourton is that many such cafes utilise beautiful old buildings of typical Cotswold design, giving the visitor a chance to view the interior as well as the outside.

BOURTON-ON-THE-WATER, THE STUDIO CAFE c1955 B392054

Traditional English teashops reached their zenith in the peaceful days of the 1950s, having made a comeback after the restrictions and rationing of the Second World War. The neat layout, the ornaments and the rack of postcards - some, perhaps, are Friths - set a standard common to the Cotswolds even up to the present day.

BROADWAY, THE VILLAGE AND THE NEW CHURCH 1899 44115

Broadway is a tempting village for tourists, full of antique and craft shops. But its popularity does nothing to detract from the fact that this is an exceptionally beautiful Cotswold village, each building in harmony with its neighbour and all constructed from the same warm local stone.

BROADWAY, THE VILLAGE 1899 44113

A number of the old houses here were originally inns, for Broadway lay on the London to Worcester coaching route. Here we can see the village in quieter days, before the constant stream of cars that flood into Broadway today; the heaviest traffic is a horse-drawn covered wagon.

BROADWAY, TUDOR HOUSE 1899 44116

Broadway has its place in history. Both Charles I and Oliver Cromwell stayed in the village during the Civil War. In the 19th century the eccentric General Lygon planted trees on his estate to match the formations of the troops at the Battle of Waterloo. In his spare time he would re-enact that famous fight.

BROADWAY, CHINA SQUARE 44117
This tumbledown cottage shows the reality of cottage life in the 19th century, far removed from the romantic restorations that we see today.

BROADWAY, THE VILLAGE c1955 B222060
By the 1950s, with the advent of popular motoring, Broadway was starting to attract car-borne tourists in considerable numbers. At about the same time many of the local shops were transformed into cafes and gift shops to cater for this new clientele.

BURFORD, HIGH STREET c1955 B369011
Sloping gently down to the River Windrush, Burford's High Street is lined with a wonderful variety of old buildings. The discerning visitor with a taste for architecture will wander off into the neighbouring streets - such as Sheep Street - to see Cotswold buildings of the very highest quality.

BURFORD, HIGH STREET c1960 B369020

Burford has not always been the peaceful place we see today. In 752 AD the Saxons defeated the Mercians in a fierce fight in the field close to the church now known as Battle Edge. In the Civil War Oliver Cromwell and Sir Thomas Fairfax incarcerated 340 mutinous troopers in Burford church. Three were later executed by firing squad in the churchyard, and a fourth was made to preach a sermon of repentance, which he did 'howling and weeping like a crocodile'.

CHIPPING CAMDEN, HIGH STREET c1955 C335035

Take away the motor cars and we have a good idea of how an affluent wool town would have looked during the 14th and 15th centuries. Grevel House, in nearby Grevel Street, belonged to the prosperous wool merchant William Grevel, supposedly the model for the merchant in Chaucer's 'Canterbury Tales'.

CHIPPING NORTON, MARKET PLACE c1948 C288010

CHIPPING NORTON
Market Place c1948

One of the highest towns in Oxfordshire, Chipping Norton gets the 'Chipping' in its name from the Saxon word for market. Its prosperity dates back to at least the 13th century, though a village stood on this site long before that. Locals rarely call the place anything but 'Chippy'.

◆

CHIPPING NORTON
Church Street c1955

The present church of St Mary's dates back to the 14th and 15th centuries, with some earlier Norman features. Church Street has eight attractive gabled almshouses, with eight front doors but nine chimneys, dating from 1640.

CHIPPING NORTON, CHURCH STREET c1955 C288020

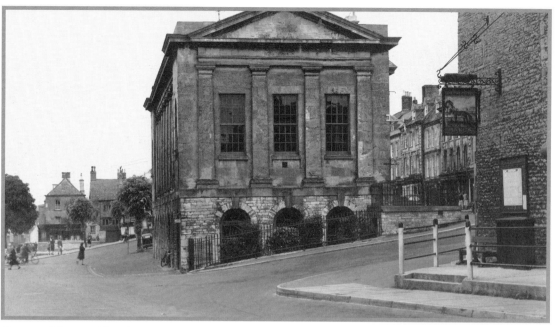

CHIPPING NORTON, THE TOWN HALL c1955 C288025

Chipping Norton's Market Square is dominated by this dramatic 19th century Town Hall. Locals and visitors come from far and wide to sample the delights of Chippy's Wednesday market which is held here - much as people have done for centuries.

CHIPPING NORTON, CHURCH STREET c1955 C288032

Chipping Norton's church was rebuilt during the days of wool trade prosperity. Legend says that a priest in olden times evicted five devils from the building, pursuing them up to the Market place and into a flock of sheep. Their five hideous faces gaze down from the vaulted ceiling of the magnificent church porch.

CHIPPING NORTON, HIGH STREET c1955 C288037

The wide central square shows Chipping Norton's origins as a market town. It is still set out with stalls on market days. By the 1950s the town had to cope with increasing traffic, and the square provided a handy solution before the construction of purpose-built car parks.

CHIPPING NORTON, NEW STREET c1955 C288043

Chipping Norton was rapidly brought under the Norman yoke in the days following the Conquest. A motte and bailey castle stood behind the site of the present church, no doubt designed to guard the important highways near-by and to intimidate the Saxons in the village below.

CHIPPING NORTON, BLISS TWEED MILLS C1960 C288051

A wonderful example of Victorian architecture, the Bliss Tweed Mills dominate the approach to Chipping Norton, looking more like a stately home than a factory. The mill was built by George Woodhouse in 1872, on the site of a mill at least a hundred years older. The business continued in operation until 1980; the building has since been converted into luxury apartments.

CHURCHILL, THE VILLAGE AND THE CHURCH C1960 C290003

Just south of Chipping Norton is the handsome church tower of the appropriately-named village of Churchill; the tower is a copy of the tower at Magdalen College, Oxford. This quiet village was the birthplace of Warren Hastings, governor-general of India, whose trial and acquittal on charges of corruption was one of the longest legal proceedings in British history.

CHURCHILL, THE CHURCH c1960 C290001
In 1769 William Smith was born in a house in Churchill which still survives. Smith produced the first geological map showing England's rock structure, and he is considered to be the father of modern geology.

CHURCHILL, THE COTSWOLDS FROM THE VILLAGE c1960 C290002
A fine Frith panorama of the Cotswolds seen from near the village of Churchill, showing the unspoiled nature of this beautiful stretch of the Oxfordshire countryside. In the Middle Ages thousands of sheep would have grazed these high wolds and sweeping meadows, providing the wool for countless mills and cottage weavers.

CORNWELL, THE VILLAGE c1965 C720049

Nestled in a fold of the Cotswolds, the neat village of Cornwell is one of a piece with the beautiful stone manor house just to the west, providing a unified design rare in Oxfordshire. The manor was restored in the 20th century by Clough Williams-Ellis, the celebrated architect of Portmeirion.

CORNWELL, THE VILLAGE c1965 C720062

Given the lack of car parking (and who would wish to blight such a perfect spot with parked cars anyway?) the best way to visit Cornwell is to walk or cycle there from Chipping Norton. There are a number of delightful country lanes to explore in the vicinity, where it is possible to get a real feel for the gentle Oxfordshire countryside.

HAILES, FROM THE EAST 1924 76164

HAILES
From the East 1924

Little remains of the 13th-century Hailes Abbey except the ruins of the cloisters. But there is a wonderfully peaceful atmosphere, and it is easy to see why the monks chose this remote site for their contemplative life. An excellent little museum on the site gives an idea of the majesty of the original buildings and shows off some of the remaining relics.

◆

HAILES
Paintings on the South Wall of the Church 1924

Visitors to Hailes Abbey should not miss the delightful little parish church, which stood long before the nearby abbey was built, and which survives the greater religious house. Edward I 'Longshanks' came here in 1301 to attend the funeral of his cousin Edmund. The King's coat of arms are still displayed in the church. The medieval wall paintings give an account of saints in a rustic setting.

HAILES, PAINTINGS ON THE SOUTH WALL OF THE CHURCH 1924 76167

LOWER SLAUGHTER, THE POST OFFICE c1955 L313007

Lower Slaughter is an artist's and photographer's paradise, with its picturesque stream flowing under attractive little stone bridges. The village's name comes not from some gruesome event in its past, but probably from the Old English word 'sclotre', meaning a muddy place.

LOWER SLAUGHTER, THE POST OFFICE c1955 L313010

Lower Slaughter is best visited on a crisp winter's day, when the stream is full and the houses stand clear against the morning sun. To see this small village in the absence of too many people is to get a feeling of how isolated these Cotswold villages would have been in earlier times.

UPPER SLAUGHTER, THE SQUARE c1960 U44004

Upper Slaughter's tiny church has been 'restored' on several occasions, not always sympathetically. But it does retain a number of interesting Norman features and a rare 14th century Sanctus Bellcot, which have managed to survive the worst excesses of the Victorian restorers.

UPPER SLAUGHTER, THE VILLAGE c1960 U44003

Upper Slaughter was the home of F E Witts, the 19th-century parson, who portrayed the village in his 'Diary of a Cotswold Parson'. Witts was a 'Squarson' of the old sort, being both the Lord of the Manor and the rector of this lovely village in its exquisite pastoral setting.

LOWER SWELL, THE VILLAGE c1955 L525011

Not far distant from the Slaughters are the little villages of Lower and Upper Swell, both situated in an entrancing rural landscape along the banks of the River Dikler. The church at Lower Swell has some fine Norman carving, and is thought to stand on an important Roman site.

UPPER SWELL, ST MARY'S CHURCH c1955 U56009

Visitors' cars are sensibly discouraged from entering the narrow lanes of Upper Swell, leaving this lovely village for the pedestrian to enjoy. St Mary's has an impressive Norman doorway and a 15th-century porch which, happily, the destructive Victorians left alone.

STOW-ON-THE-WOLD, THE GREEN c1955 S260003a
'Stow-on-the-Wold, where the wind blows cold...' runs the ancient rhyme. The highest town in the Cotswolds can certainly be windswept, particularly in the winter. On balmier days it is a good place to halt for a while. Stow is not only an attractive town, but one steeped in the riches of English history.

STOW-ON-THE-WOLD, VIEW FROM THE LYCH GATE c1955 S260047

Stow-on-the-Wold's parish church has interesting architecture dating back to the Norman Conquest. Its stained glass comes from this early Norman period, with some interesting additions by the Victorian stained glass revivalist William Wailes. The 17th-century painter de Craeyer, a pupil of Rubens, produced the colourful depiction of the crucifixion that adorns the building.

STOW-ON-THE-WOLD, THE SQUARE AND THE STOCKS c1955 S260010

The English Civil War ended at Stow-on-the-Wold when the parliamentarian Sir William Brereton defeated the aged royalist Sir Jacob Astley in 1646. Some 1600 prisoners were incarcerated in the parish church of St Edward after a last fight at nearby Donnington.

STOW-ON-THE-WOLD, THE SQUARE 1957 S260045

Local lore says that the buildings were clustered so tightly around the Square to keep the wind off the farmers on market days. Daniel Defoe records in his 'Tour of Britain' that 20,000 sheep were sold at Stow-on-the-Wold market in the year prior to his visit.

STOW-ON-THE-WOLD, THE MARKET CROSS c1960 S260063
Stow-on-the-Wold is the junction of eight major roads, including the Roman Fosse Way, and has always attracted travellers from far and wide. This old market cross, with its restored lantern head, must have witnessed centuries of Stow's history.

WINCHCOMBE, THE VILLAGE 1907 59456
Winchcombe lies on the high ground to the north-east of Cheltenham; its street pattern suggests its origins as an important Saxon town, once the capital of the kingdom of Mercia. Its Saxon abbey, the burial place of the Mercian King Kenulf and his son Saint Kenelm, was destroyed during the Reformation.

WINCHCOMBE, THE JACOBEAN HOUSE AND THE CHURCH c1955 W378002

Winchcombe's long central street becomes in turn Hailes Street, High Street, Abbey Terrace, Gloucester Street and Cheltenham Road, showing off a great variety of magnificent architecture along the way. The Jacobean House in Queen Square is constructed of the same beautifully coloured stone as many of its simpler neighbours.

WINCHCOMBE, HIGH STREET c1960 W378017

Winchcombe was the final home of Henry VIII's surviving Queen Catherine Parr, who lived just south of the town at Sudeley Castle. It is unfortunate that her tomb was destroyed during the Civil War, but the town boasts an example of her needlework.

WINCHCOMBE, GLOUCESTER STREET c1955 W378006
Mingled among the Cotswold stone buildings of
Winchcombe are a number of black and white timbered
buildings, suggesting the architectural influence of the
Vale of Evesham rather than of Cotswold pure and true.

WINCHCOMBE, ST PETER'S CHURCH c1960 W378027

St Peter's Church is all that remains of the older Winchcombe Abbey, and dates from the 15th century. Many come to see the 'Winchcombe Worthies', a collection of forty grotesque gargoyles adorning the outside wall.

WINCHCOMBE, HAILES STREET c1960 W378023

The gabled George Inn, with its galleried courtyard, seen here on the left halfway up Hailes Street, dates back nearly eight hundred years when it served as a lodging house for pilgrims to the abbey. One of its lintels still bears the monogram of Richard Kidderminster, a former abbot. The 16th-century timbered house on the right was once an inn called the Sudeley Arms.

WINCHCOMBE, NORTH STREET c1960 W378019

It is probable that much of the stone from the abbey was used to construct and repair buildings in the town. Seeking out the use of salvaged building materials makes an unusual and fascinating walk - a good way to explore the quieter corners of Winchcombe.

WINCHCOMBE, VINEYARD STREET c1960 W378034

A row of Cotswold stone cottages in Vineyard Street, named after the former abbey's vineyard which was once nearby, built in the style so beloved of all who love the towns and villages of the Cotswolds - and who return again and again.

Index

Frith Book Co Titles

www.francisfrith.co.uk

The Frith Book Company publishes over 100 new titles each year. A selection of those currently available are listed below. For latest catalogue please contact Frith Book Co.

Town Books 96 pages, approx 100 photos. County and Themed Books 128 pages, approx 150 photos (unless specified). All titles hardback laminated case and jacket except those indicated pb (paperback)

Title	ISBN	Price	Title	ISBN	Price
Amersham, Chesham & Rickmansworth (pb)			Derby (pb)	1-85937-367-4	£9.99
	1-85937-340-2	£9.99	Derbyshire (pb)	1-85937-196-5	£9.99
Ancient Monuments & Stone Circles	1-85937-143-4	£17.99	Devon (pb)	1-85937-297-x	£9.99
Aylesbury (pb)	1-85937-227-9	£9.99	Dorset (pb)	1-85937-269-4	£9.99
Bakewell	1-85937-113-2	£12.99	Dorset Churches	1-85937-172-8	£17.99
Barnstaple (pb)	1-85937-300-3	£9.99	Dorset Coast (pb)	1-85937-299-6	£9.99
Bath (pb)	1-85937419-0	£9.99	Dorset Living Memories	1-85937-210-4	£14.99
Bedford (pb)	1-85937-205-8	£9.99	Down the Severn	1-85937-118-3	£14.99
Berkshire (pb)	1-85937-191-4	£9.99	Down the Thames (pb)	1-85937-278-3	£9.99
Berkshire Churches	1-85937-170-1	£17.99	Down the Trent	1-85937-311-9	£14.99
Blackpool (pb)	1-85937-382-8	£9.99	Dublin (pb)	1-85937-231-7	£9.99
Bognor Regis (pb)	1-85937-431-x	£9.99	East Anglia (pb)	1-85937-265-1	£9.99
Bournemouth	1-85937-067-5	£12.99	East London	1-85937-080-2	£14.99
Bradford (pb)	1-85937-204-x	£9.99	East Sussex	1-85937-130-2	£14.99
Brighton & Hove(pb)	1-85937-192-2	£8.99	Eastbourne	1-85937-061-6	£12.99
Bristol (pb)	1-85937-264-3	£9.99	Edinburgh (pb)	1-85937-193-0	£8.99
British Life A Century Ago (pb)	1-85937-213-9	£9.99	England in the 1880s	1-85937-331-3	£17.99
Buckinghamshire (pb)	1-85937-200-7	£9.99	English Castles (pb)	1-85937-434-4	£9.99
Camberley (pb)	1-85937-222-8	£9.99	English Country Houses	1-85937-161-2	£17.99
Cambridge (pb)	1-85937-422-0	£9.99	Essex (pb)	1-85937-270-8	£9.99
Cambridgeshire (pb)	1-85937-420-4	£9.99	Exeter	1-85937-126-4	£12.99
Canals & Waterways (pb)	1-85937-291-0	£9.99	Exmoor	1-85937-132-9	£14.99
Canterbury Cathedral (pb)	1-85937-179-5	£9.99	Falmouth	1-85937-066-7	£12.99
Cardiff (pb)	1-85937-093-4	£9.99	Folkestone (pb)	1-85937-124-8	£9.99
Carmarthenshire	1-85937-216-3	£14.99	Glasgow (pb)	1-85937-190-6	£9.99
Chelmsford (pb)	1-85937-310-0	£9.99	Gloucestershire	1-85937-102-7	£14.99
Cheltenham (pb)	1-85937-095-0	£9.99	Great Yarmouth (pb)	1-85937-426-3	£9.99
Cheshire (pb)	1-85937-271-6	£9.99	Greater Manchester (pb)	1-85937-266-x	£9.99
Chester	1-85937-090-x	£12.99	Guildford (pb)	1-85937-410-7	£9.99
Chesterfield	1-85937-378-x	£9.99	Hampshire (pb)	1-85937-279-1	£9.99
Chichester (pb)	1-85937-228-7	£9.99	Hampshire Churches (pb)	1-85937-207-4	£9.99
Colchester (pb)	1-85937-188-4	£8.99	Harrogate	1-85937-423-9	£9.99
Cornish Coast	1-85937-163-9	£14.99	Hastings & Bexhill (pb)	1-85937-131-0	£9.99
Cornwall (pb)	1-85937-229-5	£9.99	Heart of Lancashire (pb)	1-85937-197-3	£9.99
Cornwall Living Memories	1-85937-248-1	£14.99	Helston (pb)	1-85937-214-7	£9.99
Cotswolds (pb)	1-85937-230-9	£9.99	Hereford (pb)	1-85937-175-2	£9.99
Cotswolds Living Memories	1-85937-255-4	£14.99	Herefordshire	1-85937-174-4	£14.99
County Durham	1-85937-123-x	£14.99	Hertfordshire (pb)	1-85937-247-3	£9.99
Croydon Living Memories	1-85937-162-0	£9.99	Horsham (pb)	1-85937-432-8	£9.99
Cumbria	1-85937-101-9	£14.99	Humberside	1-85937-215-5	£14.99
Dartmoor	1-85937-145-0	£14.99	Hythe, Romney Marsh & Ashford	1-85937-256-2	£9.99

Available from your local bookshop or from the publisher

Frith Book Co Titles (continued)

Title	ISBN	Price	Title	ISBN	Price
Ipswich (pb)	1-85937-424-7	£9.99	St Ives (pb)	1-85937415-8	£9.99
Ireland (pb)	1-85937-181-7	£9.99	Scotland (pb)	1-85937-182-5	£9.99
Isle of Man (pb)	1-85937-268-6	£9.99	Scottish Castles (pb)	1-85937-323-2	£9.99
Isles of Scilly	1-85937-136-1	£14.99	Sevenoaks & Tunbridge	1-85937-057-8	£12.99
Isle of Wight (pb)	1-85937-429-8	£9.99	Sheffield, South Yorks (pb)	1-85937-267-8	£9.99
Isle of Wight Living Memories	1-85937-304-6	£14.99	Shrewsbury (pb)	1-85937-325-9	£9.99
Kent (pb)	1-85937-189-2	£9.99	Shropshire (pb)	1-85937-326-7	£9.99
Kent Living Memories	1-85937-125-6	£14.99	Somerset	1-85937-153-1	£14.99
Lake District (pb)	1-85937-275-9	£9.99	South Devon Coast	1-85937-107-8	£14.99
Lancaster, Morecambe & Heysham (pb)	1-85937-233-3	£9.99	South Devon Living Memories	1-85937-168-x	£14.99
Leeds (pb)	1-85937-202-3	£9.99	South Hams	1-85937-220-1	£14.99
Leicester	1-85937-073-x	£12.99	Southampton (pb)	1-85937-427-1	£9.99
Leicestershire (pb)	1-85937-185-x	£9.99	Southport (pb)	1-85937-425-5	£9.99
Lincolnshire (pb)	1-85937-433-6	£9.99	Staffordshire	1-85937-047-0	£12.99
Liverpool & Merseyside (pb)	1-85937-234-1	£9.99	Stratford upon Avon	1-85937-098-5	£12.99
London (pb)	1-85937-183-3	£9.99	Suffolk (pb)	1-85937-221-x	£9.99
Ludlow (pb)	1-85937-176-0	£9.99	Suffolk Coast	1-85937-259-7	£14.99
Luton (pb)	1-85937-235-x	£9.99	Surrey (pb)	1-85937-240-6	£9.99
Maidstone	1-85937-056-x	£14.99	Sussex (pb)	1-85937-184-1	£9.99
Manchester (pb)	1-85937-198-1	£9.99	Swansea (pb)	1-85937-167-1	£9.99
Middlesex	1-85937-158-2	£14.99	Tees Valley & Cleveland	1-85937-211-2	£14.99
New Forest	1-85937-128-0	£14.99	Thanet (pb)	1-85937-116-7	£9.99
Newark (pb)	1-85937-366-6	£9.99	Tiverton (pb)	1-85937-178-7	£9.99
Newport, Wales (pb)	1-85937-258-9	£9.99	Torbay	1-85937-063-2	£12.99
Newquay (pb)	1-85937-421-2	£9.99	Truro	1-85937-147-7	£12.99
Norfolk (pb)	1-85937-195-7	£9.99	Victorian and Edwardian Cornwall	1-85937-252-x	£14.99
Norfolk Living Memories	1-85937-217-1	£14.99	Victorian & Edwardian Devon	1-85937-253-8	£14.99
Northamptonshire	1-85937-150-7	£14.99	Victorian & Edwardian Kent	1-85937-149-3	£14.99
Northumberland Tyne & Wear (pb)	1-85937-281-3	£9.99	Vic & Ed Maritime Album	1-85937-144-2	£17.99
North Devon Coast	1-85937-146-9	£14.99	Victorian and Edwardian Sussex	1-85937-157-4	£14.99
North Devon Living Memories	1-85937-261-9	£14.99	Victorian & Edwardian Yorkshire	1-85937-154-x	£14.99
North London	1-85937-206-6	£14.99	Victorian Seaside	1-85937-159-0	£17.99
North Wales (pb)	1-85937-298-8	£9.99	Villages of Devon (pb)	1-85937-293-7	£9.99
North Yorkshire (pb)	1-85937-236-8	£9.99	Villages of Kent (pb)	1-85937-294-5	£9.99
Norwich (pb)	1-85937-194-9	£8.99	Villages of Sussex (pb)	1-85937-295-3	£9.99
Nottingham (pb)	1-85937-324-0	£9.99	Warwickshire (pb)	1-85937-203-1	£9.99
Nottinghamshire (pb)	1-85937-187-6	£9.99	Welsh Castles (pb)	1-85937-322-4	£9.99
Oxford (pb)	1-85937-411-5	£9.99	West Midlands (pb)	1-85937-289-9	£9.99
Oxfordshire (pb)	1-85937-430-1	£9.99	West Sussex	1-85937-148-5	£14.99
Peak District (pb)	1-85937-280-5	£9.99	West Yorkshire (pb)	1-85937-201-5	£9.99
Penzance	1-85937-069-1	£12.99	Weymouth (pb)	1-85937-209-0	£9.99
Peterborough (pb)	1-85937-219-8	£9.99	Wiltshire (pb)	1-85937-277-5	£9.99
Piers	1-85937-237-6	£17.99	Wiltshire Churches (pb)	1-85937-171-x	£9.99
Plymouth	1-85937-119-1	£12.99	Wiltshire Living Memories	1-85937-245-7	£14.99
Poole & Sandbanks (pb)	1-85937-251-1	£9.99	Winchester (pb)	1-85937-428-x	£9.99
Preston (pb)	1-85937-212-0	£9.99	Windmills & Watermills	1-85937-242-2	£17.99
Reading (pb)	1-85937-238-4	£9.99	Worcester (pb)	1-85937-165-5	£9.99
Romford (pb)	1-85937-319-4	£9.99	Worcestershire	1-85937-152-3	£14.99
Salisbury (pb)	1-85937-239-2	£9.99	York (pb)	1-85937-199-x	£9.99
Scarborough (pb)	1-85937-379-8	£9.99	Yorkshire (pb)	1-85937-186-8	£9.99
St Albans (pb)	1-85937-341-0	£9.99	Yorkshire Living Memories	1-85937-166-3	£14.99

See Frith books on the internet www.francisfrith.co.uk

FRITH PRODUCTS & SERVICES

Francis Frith would doubtless be pleased to know that the pioneering publishing venture he started in 1860 still continues today. A hundred and forty years later, The Francis Frith Collection continues in the same innovative tradition and is now one of the foremost publishers of vintage photographs in the world. Some of the current activities include:

Interior Decoration

Today Frith's photographs can be seen framed and as giant wall murals in thousands of pubs, restaurants, hotels, banks, retail stores and other public buildings throughout the country. In every case they enhance the unique local atmosphere of the places they depict and provide reminders of gentler days in an increasingly busy and frenetic world.

Product Promotions

Frith products are used by many major companies to promote the sales of their own products or to reinforce their own history and heritage. Frith promotions have been used by Hovis bread, Courage beers, Scots Porage Oats, Colman's mustard, Cadbury's foods, Mellow Birds coffee, Dunhill pipe tobacco, Guinness, and Bulmer's Cider.

Genealogy and Family History

As the interest in family history and roots grows world-wide, more and more people are turning to Frith's photographs of Great Britain for images of the towns, villages and streets where their ancestors lived; and, of course, photographs of the churches and chapels where their ancestors were christened, married and buried are an essential part of every genealogy tree and family album.

Frith Products

All Frith photographs are available Framed or just as Mounted Prints and Posters (size 23 x 16 inches). These may be ordered from the address below. From time to time other products - Address Books, Calendars, Table Mats, etc - are available.

The Internet

Already twenty thousand Frith photographs can be viewed and purchased on the internet through the Frith websites and a myriad of partner sites.

For more detailed information on Frith companies and products, look at these sites:

www.francisfrith.co.uk
www.francisfrith.com
(for North American visitors)

See the complete list of Frith Books at:

www.francisfrith.co.uk

This web site is regularly updated with the latest list of publications from the Frith Book Company. If you wish to buy books relating to another part of the country that your local bookshop does not stock, you may purchase on-line.

For further information, trade, or author enquiries please contact us at the address below:
The Francis Frith Collection, Frith's Barn, Teffont, Salisbury, Wiltshire, England SP3 5QP.
Tel: +44 (0)1722 716 376 Fax: +44 (0)1722 716 881 Email: sales@francisfrith.co.uk

See Frith books on the internet www.francisfrith.co.uk

TO RECEIVE YOUR **FREE** MOUNTED PRINT

Mounted Print
Overall size 14 x 11 inches

Cut out this Voucher and return it with your remittance for £1.95 to cover postage and handling, to UK addresses. For overseas addresses please include £4.00 post and handling. Choose any photograph included in this book. Your SEPIA print will be A4 in size, and mounted in a cream mount with burgundy rule line, overall size 14 x 11 inches.

Order additional Mounted Prints at HALF PRICE (only £7.49 each*)

If there are further pictures you would like to order, possibly as gifts for friends and family, purchase them at half price (no additional postage and handling required).

Have your Mounted Prints framed*

For an additional £14.95 per print you can have your chosen Mounted Print framed in an elegant polished wood and gilt moulding, overall size 16 x 13 inches (no additional postage and handling required).

> *** IMPORTANT!**
> These special prices are only available if ordered using the original voucher on this page (no copies permitted) and at the same time as your free Mounted Print, for delivery to the same address

Frith Collectors' Guild

From time to time we publish a magazine of news and stories about Frith photographs and further special offers of Frith products. If you would like 12 months FREE membership, please return this form.

Send completed forms to:
The Francis Frith Collection, Frith's Barn, Teffont, Salisbury, Wiltshire SP3 5QP

Voucher for **FREE** and Reduced Price Frith Prints

Picture no.	Page number	Qty	Mounted @ £7.49	Framed + £14.95	Total Cost
		1	**Free of charge***	£	£
			£7.49	£	£
			£7.49	£	£
			£7.49	£	£
			£7.49	£	£
			£7.49	£	£

Please allow 28 days for delivery	*** Post & handling**	**£1.95**
Book Title	**Total Order Cost**	**£**

Please do not photocopy this voucher. Only the original is valid, so please cut it out and return it to us.

I enclose a cheque / postal order for £ . . . .
made payable to 'The Francis Frith Collection'
OR please debit my Mastercard / Visa / Switch / Amex card
(credit cards please on all overseas orders)

Number . . . .

Issue No (Switch only) . . . . Valid from (Amex/Switch) . . . .

Expires . . . . Signature . . . .

Name Mr/Mrs/Ms . . . .

Address . . . .

. . . .

. . . . Postcode . . . .

Daytime Tel No . . . . Valid to 31/12/02

The Francis Frith Collectors' Guild

Please enrol me as a member for 12 months free of charge.

Name Mr/Mrs/Ms . . . .

Address . . . .

. . . .

. . . .

. . . . Postcode . . . .

Would you like to find out more about Francis Frith?

We have recently recruited some entertaining speakers who are happy to visit local groups, clubs and societies to give an illustrated talk documenting Frith's travels and photographs. If you are a member of such a group and are interested in hosting a presentation, we would love to hear from you.

Our speakers bring with them a small selection of our local town and county books, together with sample prints. They are happy to take orders. A small proportion of the order value is donated to the group who have hosted the presentation. The talks are therefore an excellent way of fundraising for small groups and societies.

Can you help us with information about any of the Frith photographs in this book?

We are gradually compiling an historical record for each of the photographs in the Frith archive. It is always fascinating to find out the names of the people shown in the pictures, as well as insights into the shops, buildings and other features depicted.

If you recognize anyone in the photographs in this book, or if you have information not already included in the author's caption, do let us know. We would love to hear from you, and will try to publish it in future books or articles.

Our production team

Frith books are produced by a small dedicated team at offices in the converted Grade II listed 18th-century barn at Teffont near Salisbury, illustrated above. Most have worked with the Frith Collection for many years. All have in common one quality: they have a passion for the Frith Collection. The team is constantly expanding, but currently includes:

Jason Buck, John Buck, Douglas Burns, Heather Crisp, Isobel Hall, Rob Hames, Hazel Heaton, Peter Horne, James Kinnear, Tina Leary, Hannah Marsh, Eliza Sackett, Terence Sackett, Sandra Sanger, Shelley Tolcher, Susanna Walker, Clive Wathen and Jenny Wathen.

Free Print - see overleaf